Loving
Changes

a journal for
mothers in times
of transition

Loving
Changes

LYNNE MOBBERLEY DEMING
KATHLEEN CROCKFORD ACKLEY

The Pilgrim Press
Cleveland, Ohio

The Pilgrim Press, Cleveland, Ohio 44115

Printed in Hong Kong on acid-free paper

03 02 01 00 99 98   5 4 3 2 1

ISBN 0-8298-1239-3

We dedicate this book to David J. Deming, Daniel R. Deming, Christy E. Ackley, and Brian F. Ackley—the amazing human beings who have most intimately shaped our lives as parents and persons. We celebrate your spirit and your love throughout the transitions.

Sometimes ideas for projects emerge from a need that we feel personally. So it is with *Loving Changes: A Journal for Mothers in Times of Transition*. Recently, we both experienced the pangs of saying goodbye to our children as they ventured forth to college and into the working world. As we wrote in our journals about this significant time of transition, it was clear that the feelings we felt were unique to the circumstances. And yet there was something familiar about them as well. Throughout the parenting years there have been little "goodbyes"—times when we have encouraged our children to grow, stretch, risk—preceding these "loving changes."

When we told others about the project, one friend remembered wistfully the exhilarating moment when her son found his own balance on his bicycle and rode off for the first time without a grownup hand to steady him. "It was so exciting to see him move forward on his own, but I remember thinking, 'He is really on his own now; he's not looking back.' It was such a powerful metaphor for coming to understand that he would be independent someday, sooner than I would think."

Perhaps this journal is all about providing a space where we, as mothers, as people, can find our balance in changing times. Whether we are expecting a child, sending one to school for the first time, or living the drama of our child's transformation from childhood to adolescence, journaling can help us sift through our feelings and bring balance to life when the world around us is shifting.

We hope that you will find encouragement, comfort, wisdom, and balance as you read the words of the women who are quoted in these pages and contemplate the artwork by and about mothers. We hope, too, that your own words will reveal to you the many ways in which your loving changes you as you travel the path of motherhood.

LYNNE MOBBERLEY DEMING
KATHLEEN CROCKFORD ACKLEY

■

Loving
Changes

week  1

monday
lunes
montag
lundi

Marilyn C. Szalay, *Waiting,*

© 1983, photograph

■

Life is a series of letting go's. Each new stage has its
own birthing with the joys and pains that follow.

—MARIA HARRIS

1

It's a good thing to have
all the props pulled out
from under us occasion-
ally. It gives us some
sense of what is rock
under our feet, and what
is sand.

—MADELEINE L'ENGLE

■

Women don't stop caring for children when they start
cooking dinner. . . . Doing a task like shelling peas or
raking the lawn alongside a child often makes for a
deeper companionship than stripping the moment down
to a single focus on relationship.

—MARY CATHERINE BATESON

4

Stepparents and stepchildren
often experience a push and
pull—wanting trust to develop
fast and yet being scared of
getting close too quickly.

—NANCY PRESS HAWLEY

saturday

sábado

samstag

samedi

■

For those of us who have raised families, being a mother was probably one of our most absorbing, time-consuming, and demanding relationships.

—PAULA B. DORESS-WORTERS AND

DIANA LASKIN SIEGAL

6

There *is* a secret communion

between women who literally

hold new life within them, a

curious shared wonder

exchanged in a passing

glance.

—WENDY M. WRIGHT

Janet Century, *Victoria and*

Brandon, © 1998, photograph

■

Nothing can replace creativity in our lives—not work, not love, not children, nothing. We may be creative in all these areas, yet our creative impulses must find their own avenue for expression.

—ANNE WILSON SCHAEF

wednesday

miércoles

mittwoch

mercredi

2

Children give me particu-

lar hope because they

have more open minds.

—JANE GOODALL

11

thursday

jueves

donnerstag

jeudi

■

Once we become parents, whether through pregnancy
and childbirth, adoption or stepparenthood, we have
made a decision that will produce countless changes in
our lives.

—RUTH DAVIDSON BELL

Considering ourselves more fully as people has allowed us to see our children as people.

—WENDY COPPEDGE SANFORD

2

There is a deep hurt that I feel as a mother. Some days
it is a feeling of futility.

—ALICE WALKER

I felt a deep commitment to
providing the kind of home
where he would feel free to
bring his friends, where they
could have privacy and a
sense of ease, and where
their conversations alone
and with adults could flow
freely on any topic.

—CAROLINA MANCUSO

2

week **3**

Deborah Pinter, *Bewail,* © 1996,

photograph

17

■

_____

_____

_____

_____

_____

_____

_____

_____

_____

_____

_____

_____

_____

_____

_____

_____

_____

_____

_____

_____

Certainly we are not meant to recognize pregnancy as

the only divine role for women.

—JANN CATHER WEAVER

wednesday

miércoles

mittwoch

mercredi

3

Our heritage is

our power.

—JUDY CHICAGO

19

For a woman, the problem of finding and maintaining
the boundary between self and a loved other is
paramount.

—LILLIAN RUBIN

A way through doubt is to learn
to wait well, let our souls wait,
teach them how to wait well.

—DONNA E. SCHAPER

3

■

Raising children does involve the transmission of
continuities, but it also requires sustained and loving
attention that welcomes particularity.

—MARY CATHERINE BATESON

A child's knowledge of

nostalgia is one of the

mysteries of childhood.

—REBECCA GOLDSTEIN

3

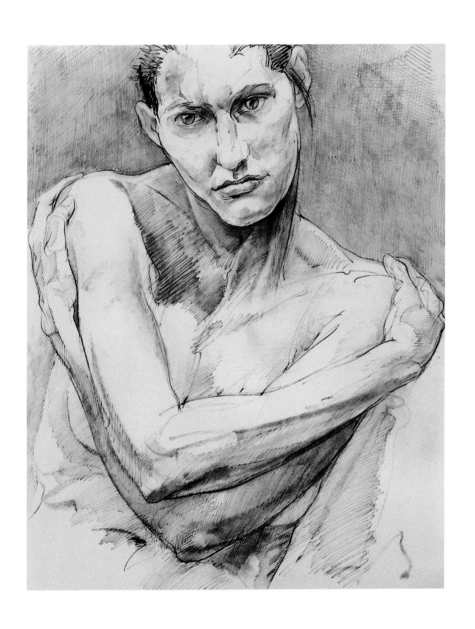

week **4**

Marilyn C. Szalay,

Embracing a Sense of Self, © 1996,

charcoal on paper

As truly as God is our Father, so truly is God our Mother.

—Julian of Norwich

4

I have never conceived,
but whether or not a
woman does conceive,
she carries the germina-
tive ocean within her, and
the essential eggs. We
have a spirituality, full
from within.

    —MEINRAD CRAIGHEAD

thursday
jueves
donnerstag
jeudi

■

I think we all eventually learned that being in the eye of
the storm is easier than observing it.

—ROSALYNN CARTER

Weeping women, women whose hearts moan like a flute because those they love have come to harm, are everywhere in the world.

—Elizabeth A. Johnson

4

I have really hated disappointing everyone, but thus far motherhood has been the richest, most satisfying of rewards.

—PATRICIA J. WILLIAMS

Just as we groom our boys

for teamwork and leader-

ship, we must help our girls

develop their inner strength

as they rise to positions of

power and influence.

—ELLEN FARMER

4

Betsy Molnar, *Florica with Marius,*

© 1997, photograph

■

We are called to express, embody, share, celebrate the
gift of life, and to pass it on!

—BEVERLY WILDUNG HARRISON

5

The caregiver is aware of
being connected to the
heart of all beings.
—ELIZABETH DODSON GRAY

■

We discover our need for inner guidance and strength,

for spiritual nurture during times of transition.

—ELAINE M. WARD

Studies of working mothers

confirm that, critical voices to

the contrary, they value their

children and their role as

mothers as much as women who

have no careers. It is simply

their definition of the role that

is different.

—CAROLE KLEIN

5

■

Feelings of worth can only flourish in an atmosphere where individual differences are appreciated, mistakes are tolerated, communication is open, and rules are flexible.

—VIRGINIA SATIR

God never tires of scooping

you up in times of failure or

discouragement . . . that is

God's immense delight!

—JANE MARIE THIBAULT

Janet Century, *Forest Hill Park Jazz,*

© 1996, photograph

tuesday
martes
dienstag
mardi

■

A woman's work is never done because, although a particular task may be completed, she is always engaged in multiple tasks, long- and short-term, cycled and recycled, and there is never a moment when she can say that no task is waiting.

—MARY CATHERINE BATESON

42

6

To realize our goals,

we must first imagine

them fully.

  —SIEW HWA BEH

■

As a mother comforts her child,

so shall I comfort you;

you will be comforted in Jerusalem.

—ISAIAH 66:13

I would be most content if my children grew up to be the kind of people who think decorating consists mostly of building enough bookshelves.

—ANNA QUINDLEN

6

■

No matter how intimately a woman makes her being one with the baby growing within her, the baby shapes her life even more than she does herself.

—ANN BELFORD ULANOV

Ancient American Indian

wisdom tells us to make

every decision in light of

its effect upon seven

generations. Too often we,

in our heedlessness, rush

headlong into actions that

threaten our children's very

existence.

—JOAN SOLOMON

week **7**

Marilyn C. Szalay, *A Question of*

the Future, © 1982, photograph

In a society that expects workers to give 150 percent dedication to the job, and considers motherhood a terrible detriment to productivity, it was incredibly stressful and even painful at times to experience such a personal conflict in a very public setting when the two worlds collided.

—JEANNINE OUELLOETTE HOWITZ

7

Scouting the terrain of the
land of aging in which we
now dwell, we recognize
that this land poses new
questions, provoked not
by the past but by the
decades ahead. "What
remains for me to do?"

—MARIA HARRIS

■

To describe my mother would be to write about a
hurricane in its perfect power.

—MAYA ANGELOU

When we look back and regret, we are indulging in the self-centered activity of beating ourselves over the mistakes in our past.

—ANNE WILSON SCHAEF

7

saturday

sábado

samstag

samedi

■

Who and where are you in this lifelong process of being

someone's child and, perhaps, someone's parent?

—WENDY COPPEDGE SANFORD

54

Can you identify someone
who challenges you to grow
without invading your
space? Who? How?

—MARJORY ZOET BANKSON

week

8

monday
lunes
montag
lundi

Nanette Yannuzzi Maciás,

Umbilicus: Remnants and

Huaraches, detail from installation,

© 1996, sumi ink on piano rolls

■

God's maternal solicitude is for us love's hidden ground.

—WENDY M. WRIGHT

8

Children, in their happy
irrationality and complete
dependence, are perpet-
ual reminders that we are
all members of a larger
community.

—PATRICIA J. WILLIAMS

The sun is shining out there, I want to get out, go some-place, exhaust myself at something beyond laundry and Candyland.

—MARY BETH DANIELSON

friday

viernes

freitag

vendredi

Joy anchors itself deeply, estab-
lishes roots, and endures in the
worst circumstances alongside
an unconquerable gladness that
no barriers can confine.

—DORIS DONNELLY

8

■

Children are perceptive observers: they watch how we treat the neighbor next door, what we do when someone pulls into a parking space in front of us, how we act when an old friend calls on the phone, what happens when a sibling breaks a dish, or when one parent arrives home late.

—NANCY PRESS HAWLEY

I don't believe motherhood
is a biological instinct in
women. . . . But it is a very
basic human potential, in
our genes and our psyches,
that does somehow demand
to be used.

—BETTY FRIEDAN

Anne Hersch, *Shirlee,* © 1997,

photograph

tuesday
martes
dienstag
mardi

■

Each soul is somebody's child, loved, dreamed for, and a promising possibility.

—GENEVA E. BELL

9

Now that I have been
loved by children who put
no conditions or limits on
their love, I could never
willingly return to living
alone.

—LAURA GREEN

thursday

jueves

donnerstag

jeudi

■

Motherhood is a profession by itself, just like school teaching and lecturing.

—IDA B. WELLS

68

Taking time for reflection is not selfishness but discovery of strength and inner resources we did not know existed.

—ELAINE M. WARD

9

In search of my mother's garden, I found my own.

—ALICE WALKER

Each of us is many women,

and each stage of life offers

the potential for discovering

new freedom, new growth,

and new pleasures.

  —PENELOPE WASHBOURN

9

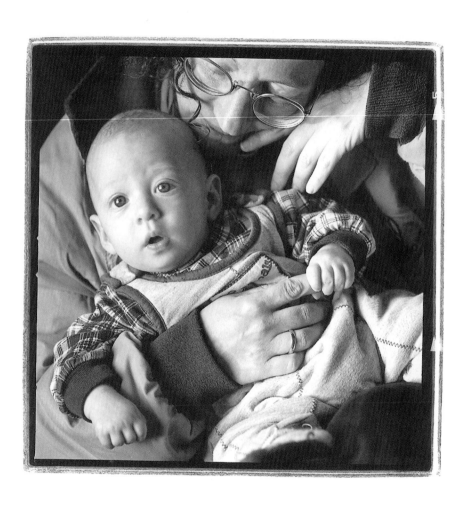

Betsy Molnar, *Janet with Peter,*

© 1995, photograph

■

Recalling childhood makes it possible to experience it again, to discover another way of seeing within one's own skin.

—MARY CATHERINE BATESON

10

Parenting forces us

to deal with our own

childhoods.

—MARY BETH DANIELSON

■

Biology is the least of what makes someone a mother.

—OPRAH WINFREY

As women, we are intimately connected to the rhythms of life and death, as we are to the rhythms of our own bodies.

—GINA FOGLIA AND DORIT WOLFFBERG

10

■

The more one gives, the more one has to give—like milk in the breast.

—ANNE MORROW LINDBERGH

Momma was home.

She was the most totally

human, human being that

I have ever known.

—LEONTYNE PRICE

10

Marilyn C. Szalay, *The Raw*

Honesty Needed to Confront

City Life, © 1985, photograph

■

The very essence of all life is growth, which means change.

—JEAN BAKER MILLER

11

All the anticipation of the
waiting and the heightened
experience of the birth day
itself are now memories,
and we are left with the
miracle in our arms and the
overwhelming sensation that
we have only just been initi-
ated into the truth of it: that
we are called to nurture
and raise to maturity what
has been given.

—WENDY M. WRIGHT

■

Our parenting, like our homemaking, is a giving
of shelter.

—PHYLLIS HARLOW

A woman's life can produce
several different harvests—each
in its appropriate season.

—NAN HUNT

11

saturday

sábado

samstag

samedi

■

God as mother is parent to *all* species and wishes all to flourish.

—SALLIE MCFAGUE

The departure of children

from home, the reduction of

job demands, and the

changes in our bodies make

us aware we're facing a

new social and biological

orientation.

—MARIA HARRIS

11

monday
lunes
montag
lundi

Sarah C. Schuster, *Fertility Series:*

Image #1, © 1990, liquid light

photo emulsion on canvas collage

■

Visualize yourself as a great mother feeding all the
beings upon this planet, sending forth loving thoughts
of peace and harmony and certainty that the crops will
be good and all will be fed.

—DHYANI YWAHOO

12

The image of God as
Mother of the whole
creation, human and
nonhuman, is an image
of inclusive love.

 —JUDITH PLASKOW AND

  CAROL P. CHRIST

■

When you are weary and without recourse, did you

ever notice that . . . some other force takes over . . .

moving you to do the impossible or the unimaginable?

—JUDY COLLINS

Change is inevitable: children
change quickly from one stage
to another, nurturing adults
never stop growing and
changing; and the world around
us never stands still.

—VIRGINIA SATIR

12

■

I'm a mom—I've been in the trenches for twenty-five
years. If you have, too, you know it's not for sissies.

—BARBARA CAWTHORNE CRAFTON

94

Women typically approach

adulthood with the under-

standing that the care and

empowerment of others

is central to their life's

work. . . . They draw out the

voices and minds of those

they help to raise up. In the

process, they often come to

hear, value, and strengthen

their own voices and minds

as well.

—MARY FIELD BELENKY ET AL.

monday
lunes
montag
lundi

Janet Century, *At the Vietnam*

Veterans Memorial Dedication,

Washington, D.C., November 13,

1982, © *1982, photograph*

■

I am a former pediatrician, and I know children have
many experiences of the sacred. Many young children
have told me about the angels or guardians that they
see watching over them.

—RACHEL NAOMI REMEN

13

Those who guide us up,
over, and around the
boulders and chasms of
our lives reveal the many
faces of God.

—JEAN M. BLOMQUIST

thursday

jueves

donnerstag

jeudi

∎

And for the three magic gifts I needed to escape the poverty of my hometown, I thank my mother, who gave me a sewing machine, a typewriter, and a suitcase.

—ALICE WALKER

Embracing age, wisdom, and detachment leads to a sense of ourselves as *mature*—grown-ups at last; as *moral*—spiritual beings who believe goodness and creativity can triumph over evil and decay; and as *agents*—human actors who've given up roles such as pretender, little-girl-lost, or earth-mother-who-can-fix-all-ills simply to be what we are: human.

—MARIA HARRIS

13

■

Women who work outside the house aren't the only women who are obsessed with work. Women who are home full-time rarely have time for themselves and their creative projects. After all, children are twenty-four hours a day.

—ANNE WILSON SCHAEF

Parents learn a lot from
their children about coping
with life.

—MURIEL SPARK

13

week **14**

monday
lunes
montag
lundi

Krissi Kahoun, *Untitled,* © 1993,

manipulated photograph

■

Sometimes a mother's anger wells up so intensely that it explodes. Sometimes her sadness is so deep that it engulfs all other joy.

—CAROLE KLEIN

14

And ar'n't I a woman?

I have borne thirteen

chilern and seen 'em

mos' all sold off into

slavery, and when I cried

out with a mother's grief,

none but Jesus heard—and

ar'n't I a woman?

     —SOJOURNER TRUTH

We are transfused into our children, and . . . feel more keenly for them than for ourselves.

—MARIE DE SÉVIGNÉ

God All-Wisdom is our Mother.

—JULIAN OF NORWICH

14

■

As parents we also feel pressured as we attempt to
sort out which comes first—taking care of children or
doing for ourselves.

—NANCY PRESS HAWLEY

Parenting is relationship,

intimacy, challenge, risk.

—ANNE BROYLES

14

week

15

Deborah Pinter, *Monument,*

© 1997, photograph

But God . . . mothers us in other ways . . . God as the one whose body feeds us; God as the one who labors and gives us new life on the cross; God whose creative activity confers life on us.

—WENDY M. WRIGHT

15

To become a parent is
birth to a new self for the
mother and father as well
as for the baby.

 —MADELEINE L'ENGLE

■

Maternity is on the face of it an unsocial experience.
The selfishness that a woman has learned to stifle or to
dissemble where she alone is concerned, blooms freely
and unashamed on behalf of her offspring.

—EMILY JAMES PUTNAM

My heart leaps when I look
into the face of my beautiful
Indian child, wrapped in the
strength of his father's arms.

—BUFFY SAINTE-MARIE

15

■

The Mothers have this memory, this pain, and we
are working for the future so that the new generations
won't live through what we've lived through, so people
won't disappear, aren't tortured or kidnapped. We
are working so that what our children wanted will
become a reality.

—JUANITA DE PARGAMENT

118

[God] did give us children

to make [our] dreams seem

worth while.

—LORRAINE HANSBERRY

15

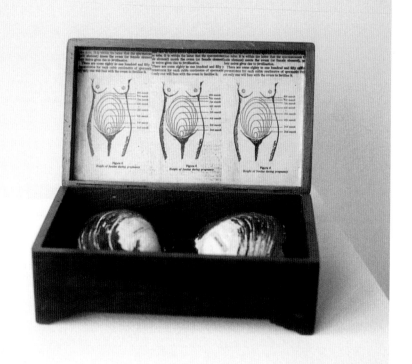

week **16**

Mona Gazala Solymos, *Summoning*

Shells, © 1996, assemblage

■

Women have not been permitted to focus on single

goals but have tended to live with ambiguity and

multiplicity. It's not easy.

—MARY CATHERINE BATESON

16

Christ's birth in the midst
of animals restores new
integrity to the whole of
creation.
—GENEVA M. BUTZ

Some of our children don't take their responsibilities to teach us seriously, but then again parents are notoriously slow learners.

—ANNE WILSON SCHAEF

Though motherhood is the
most important of all the profes-
sions—requiring more knowledge
than any other department in
human affairs—there was no
attention given to preparation
for this office.

—Elizabeth Cady Stanton

16

The desire for a comforting, comfortable relationship with our grown children is strong for many of us. Ironically, the eventual development of such a bond probably depends more than anything else on how well we *can* confront each other, and on how well we can let each other go.

—ALICE JUDSON RYERSON AND
WENDY COPPEDGE SANFORD

126

Family life is something like

an iceberg. Most people

are aware of only about

one-tenth of what is actually

going on—the tenth that

they can see and hear—and

often they think that is all

there is.

—VIRGINIA SATIR

16

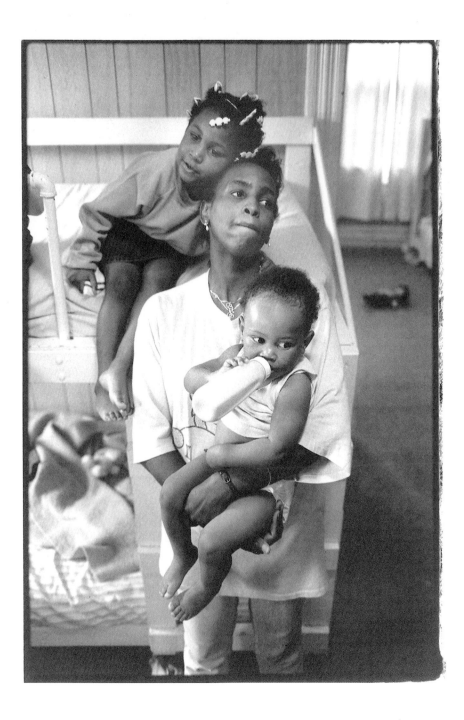

Janet Century, *Refuge at the*

Shelter, © 1990, photograph

■

The usual longevity and flexibility of women allow most of us to fulfill several roles.

—NAN HUNT

17

The deep wisdom of the
Trinity is our Mother, in
whom we are enclosed.

—JULIAN OF NORWICH

■

Children are the only future of any people. If the children's lives are squandered, and if the children . . . are not fully developed at whatever cost and sacrifice, the people will have consigned themselves to certain death.

—FRANCES CRESS WELSING

132

Mother was of royal African

blood, of a tribe ruled by

matriarchs. . . . Throughout all

her bitter years of slavery she

had managed to preserve a

queenlike dignity.

—MARY MCLEOD BETHUNE

17

∎

I was happy to have children. I had always intended to have children. . . . I wanted my body to do something its composition suggested it was supposed to do.

—GWENDOLYN BROOKS

Don't drown yourself in

busy work. That's not the

right thing. I raised children.

I traveled thousands of

miles a year. And still I

found some time for my

growth.

—ELISABETH KÜBLER-ROSS

17

Marilyn C. Szalay, *Each Day*

We Simply Grow Older, © 1982,

photograph

tuesday
martes
dienstag
mardi

■

Observe how complex is a mother's love for her

children, which draws everything toward an emotion

felt in her inmost parts.

—4 MACCABEES 14:13 (NRSV)

18

Women have long tended
the gardens of others.

—EMILY HANCOCK

■

Being a grandmother is one of the great experiences of

life, especially today, when we don't take the miracle

for granted.

—PAULA B. DORESS-WORTERS AND

DIANA LASKIN SIEGAL

There is nothing "merely biological" about this miracle of new life unless we would refuse to look with eyes of wonder upon the pulsing dynamic of the universe present in our own bodies, whose mysteries invite us to contemplate the mystery of divine life itself.

—WENDY M. WRIGHT

18

■

Considering the family as a social system—knowing that what one person does affects every other person—can make us more conscious of how our family works.

—NANCY PRESS HAWLEY

God hugs you. You are

encircled by the arms of the

mystery of God.

—HILDEGARD OF BINGEN

18

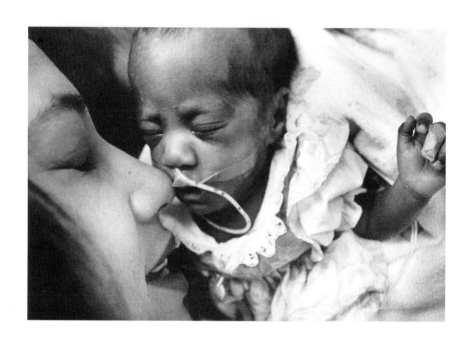

Janet Century, *Life and Love,*

© 1991, photograph

tuesday
martes
dienstag
mardi

■

Probably there is nothing in human nature more

resonant with charges than the flow of energy between

two biologically alike bodies, one of which has lain

in amniotic bliss inside the other, one of which

has laboured to give birth to the other. The materials

are here for the deepest mutuality and the most

painful estrangement.

—ADRIENNE RICH

146

19

She was nurturing within
her what had gone before
and would come after.
This child would tie her
to that past and future
as inextricably as it was
now tied to her every
heartbeat.

—GLORIA NAYLOR

■

Becoming a parent opens us to the possibility of change, for who can stay the same after giving one's heart to a child?

—ANNE BROYLES

God will feed the flock like a

shepherd, gather the lambs in

God's arms, carry them in

God's bosom, and gently lead

those that are with young.

—ISAIAH 40:11

19

saturday
sábado
samstag
samedi

■

If you wish children well, deliver them to themselves; the ultimate reward for a parent is reflected glory.

—VIVIAN AYERS-ALLEN

My dilemma is—do I myself

teach my daughter about

the world of cliques so

she'll recognize what's

going on or do I leave her

alone to fend for herself

and hope she's one of those

kids who quickly finds the

clique silly?

—ELLEN FARMER

19

week

20

monday
lunes
montag
lundi

Sarah C. Schuster, *Cocktail Dress*

for Nursing Mothers, © 1995,

lace, satin, and thread

tuesday
martes
dienstag
mardi

■

We are always making lists and eyeing the tasks that are just around the corner when we need to be working on the task at hand. Hence, rarely does anything get our full, undivided attention.

—ANNE WILSON SCHAEF

20

Even putting a bowl of
tomato soup before your
child for lunch is a sacred
act through which you
participate in life and
invest in the future of
humanity.

—RACHEL NAOMI REMEN

■

Full of confusion, I talked with her about my worries and the fear in my body. I fell on her breast, and all over again I became a little girl sobbing in her arms at the terror of life.

—GABRIELA MISTRAL

The woman with children who remarries is often inclined to treat her children as though they were her private property, thus introducing a handicap at the very beginning.

—VIRGINIA SATIR

20

Child care is a responsibility that can be shared
with other childrearers, with people who do not live with
children. This form of parenting is revolutionary in this
society . . . community-based child care.

—BELL HOOKS

In [birth] we intuitively
grasp both the awesome
wonder and responsibility of
becoming bearers of new
life as well as the great
fecundity of the creation
itself which continues to
unfold in fullness from the
poorest and most fragile of
beginnings.

  —WENDY M. WRIGHT

20

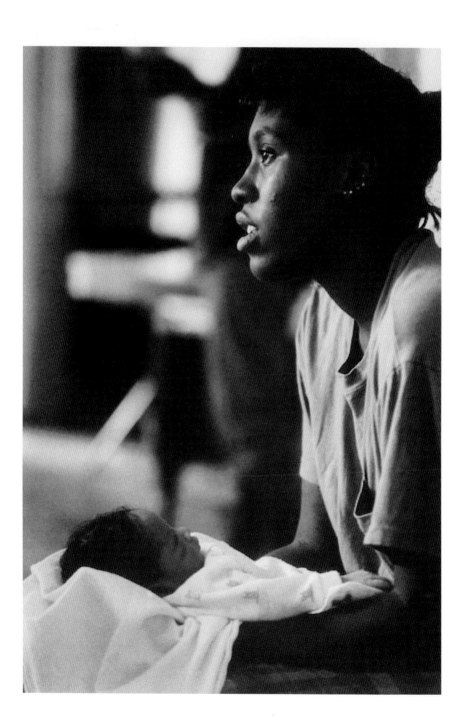

Janine Bentivegna, *Anton with*

Mother, © 1996, photograph

∎

As parents we carry around mythical ideas not only about what our families are supposed to look like, but also about how they are supposed to function. These myths might interfere with our families' ability to work as well as they might.

—NANCY PRESS HAWLEY

21

If you are parents of
worth and wisdom, train
your children so they will
be pleasing to God.

—PTAH HOTEP

thursday

jueves

donnerstag

jeudi

■

It would be so wonderful if everyone grew up under-
standing how arrogant we've been in our assumption
that the planet was created for us alone. I want children
to understand that every life—human and non-human—has
meaning and value.

—JANE GOODALL

164

I told the doctor to stop all treatment [for my son]. This was the most difficult decision I had to make in my whole life.

—GENEVA E. BELL

21

■

Moments of deep loss or failure may feel as if they have no antecedent, as if nothing like this had ever happened before in human history.

—MARY CATHERINE BATESON

166

Such a soul has the

Holy Spirit as a mother

who nurses her at the

breast of divine charity.

     —CATHERINE OF SIENA

21

week

22

Anne Hersch, *Cèline and*

Naneen, © 1997, photograph

■

In becoming young adults, our children seem to nudge us over into middle age when our self-image might not be ready for that.

—JEANNE JACOBS SPEIZER

22

Time . . . provides us with
opportunities for reflection,
for gathering up the pieces
of our lives, for weaving
them together into a sacred
whole.

—JEANNE BROOKS CARRITT

■

When you stand in a continuum of family relationships,
a mother to her daughter, a daughter to her children,
those children to their children—and this is one of the
gifts of being older—you see that every action we take
should look to future generations.

—JOAN B. CAMPBELL

When have you been a
midwife, giving support to someone who was laboring to give
birth to a dream, an idea, a
vision, a child? How have
others participated with you in
bringing something to birth?

—JAN L. RICHARDSON

22

saturday
sábado
samstag
samedi

■

You are faced with both the wonderful, frustrating, impenetrable joy and the anxiety-filled responsibility of attending to new life.

—WENDY M. WRIGHT

174

We rarely admit that carry-

ing something fragile with

you, in your hands and your

heart every minute of your

life, is one tough task.

—ANNA QUINDLEN

22

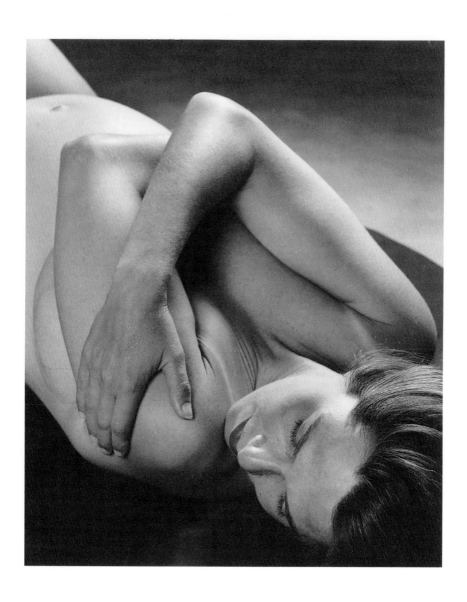

weeK

23

monday
lunes
montag
lundi

Janet Century, *Dorothy,* © 1993,

photograph

tuesday
martes
dienstag
mardi

■

We, as part of this most amazing creation, our earth,
participate in the ongoing renewal of life itself that takes
place within the structure of stars, the microbes, plant
life, and our own bodies.

—WENDY M. WRIGHT

23

We Africans take mother-

hood as the most sacred

condition human beings

can achieve.

—MAYA ANGELOU

The fine art of negotiation is one thing I hope my

children learn from living with one another.

—BARBARA MILLER

friday
viernes
freitag
vendredi

There are barriers between
women of color and white
women, but we have so much
similarity. For example, we
have children.

—CHOAU EVE LEE

23

saturday

sábado

samstag

samedi

■

Each day is a tapestry, threads of broccoli, promotions, couches, children, politics, shopping, building, planting, thinking interweave in intimate connection with insistent cycles of birth, existence, and death.

—DEENA METZGER

Embracing diversity implies

a level playing field where

all children share center

stage from time to time.

It implies mutual respect

and mutual appreciation

of a variety of cultural

experiences.

—ELLEN FARMER

23

week **24**

Marilyn C. Szalay, *A Mother's*
Memory, © 1996, charcoal, pastel,
and conté on paper

■

There are only so many hours in the day, and no one
can be in two places at once.

—MARY CATHERINE BATESON

24

By raising our children in a feminist way—from the small everyday interactions to the harder, more demanding things we do— we are making the world a more equitable place.

—DENA TAYLOR

thursday

jueves

donnerstag

jeudi

■

Like most labels applied to women's roles, "working mother" is extremely inaccurate and defeating, because it foolishly implies that there is another type of mother: the nonworking variety.

—JEANNINE OUELLOETTE HOWITZ

188

In our society, there is little
or no focused education on
parenting. We are all pretty
much on our own in the quest
for role models, beliefs and
values which will help us break
new ground.

—CAROLINA MANCUSO

24

saturday

sábado

samstag

samedi

■

> **If** I thought I had to be all and everything for my children, I could not face the task.

> —ANNE BROYLES

190

I can make something out
of [the] children. . . . They
have the essence of great-
ness in them.

    —ZORA NEALE HURSTON

24

monday
lunes
montag
lundi

Janet Century, *Christina and David,*

© 1994, photograph

■

Made in the image of God, we love as we are loved.

—ELAINE M. WARD

25

Our actions represent our

spirit. Watch a child skip

or an adult sing. We act

out of a need to connect,

to share our humanity.

    —ALEXANDRA STODDARD

■

There are as many different experiences of birth as there are women, but for all of them the waiting is over. The promised one bursts forth, new life sings out, the primal rush of blood and water carries the miracle into our arms.

—WENDY M. WRIGHT

My mother wanted me to
be a star and I worked hard
for her goal.

—LENA HORNE

25

■

No one expects to protect children from the violence in
life. However, to protect them from the glorification
of violence and to deny parental *approval* of weapons
as tools of power is a parent's right and obligation.

—LETTY COTTIN POGREBIN

Our lives are not set in
stone. Lives, like flowers,
continue to unfold. We
have options and we have
choices all along the way.

—ANNE WILSON SCHAEF

25

Janet Century, *Home Care*, © 1989,

photograph

Yet you, O God, are the one who took me from the womb;
you kept me safe upon my mother's breasts. Upon you I
was cast from my birth, and since my mother bore me you
have been my God.

—PSALM 22:9-10

26

My ole mammy would
sit . . . an' look up at the
stars an' groan. . . .
"Mammy, what makes
you groan so?" . . . "I'm
groanin' to think o' my
poor children: they
don't know where I be,
an' I don't know where
they be."

—SOJOURNER TRUTH

I'll be with you always, even when you don't want
me to be.

—DIANA ROSS

As it is with all parents, there
were choices I had to make
along the way. Directions I had
to go so that my son would
have influences that I felt were
better for him.

—ANNE MACKENZIE

26

∎

I believe parenting is too big and too important a job

for one person, or even two, to take on by themselves.

I am grateful for the friends and family members in

our lives.

—DENA TAYLOR

Only if children grow up

with a respect for living

things will the planet have a

chance for survival.

—JANE GOODALL

26

27

Janet Century, *Nancy and Jamie,*

© 1997, photograph

■

We can carry on the process of learning in everything

we do, like a mother balancing her child on one hip as

she goes about her work with the other hand or uses it

to open the doors of the unknown.

—MARY CATHERINE BATESON

27

We must consider the
effects our acts and
desires will have on those
who come after us.

—IRENE STOCK

■

Loving others is a quality of one's own heart.

—SIMONE WEIL

To the property of motherhood

belong nature, love, wisdom

and knowledge, and this is God.

—JULIAN OF NORWICH

27

■

We did *try* to warn him . . . that taking stands could get you in trouble and cost you friends. . . . I remember him coming home crying about it . . . I remember holding him tightly, crying myself, while I murmured over and over that no one could fight on every front every minute, that you had to be selective.

—ROBIN MORGAN

We cannot be with our

children all the time, nor do

we want to be, but we are

unavoidably aware that

they are living in an often

more dangerous and com-

plicated world than the one

we knew.

    —JEANNE JACOBS SPEIZER

27

week **28**

Sarah C. Schuster, *Fertility Series:*

Image #2, © 1990, liquid light

photo emulsion on canvas collage

■

We women who do too much have a terrible time loving the moment.

—ANNE WILSON SCHAEF

28

Aging means living in the
interstices of paradoxes:
doing and not-doing,
laughing and weeping,
living and dying.

   —MARIA HARRIS

■

I urge you to try it if you want to recapture the free child that you once were. Let go of the stress. Take time in your busy world to quiet the mind.

—ARDATH RODALE

The "godmother network" is an idea playwright Glenda Dickerson shared with me a few years ago. When her teenage daughter was having a difficult time with her "coming of age," Glenda found other women to help her ease the child through it. This is the way of most indigenous tribal people.

—ELENA FEATHERSTON

28

■

Adolescence is a tough time for parent and child alike.
It is a time between: between childhood and maturity,
between parental protection and personal responsibility,
between life stage managed by grown-ups and life
privately held.

—ANNA QUINDLEN

No matter how well we
know our children, as
parents, we also realize that
there are depths in their
interior lives that we will
never begin to know.

—ANNE BROYLES

28

29

Janet Century, *Nostalgia*, © 1978,

photograph

To me, my mother's English is perfectly clear, perfectly natural. It's my mother tongue. Her language, as I hear it, is vivid, direct, full of observation and imagery. That was the language that helped shape the way I saw things, expressed things, made sense of the world.

—AMY TAN

29

A new biological mother
finds support and nurture
for her changing identity
in the circle of friends and
loved ones who care for
and encourage her.

    —WENDY M. WRIGHT

∎

Our children are changing and maturing in a myriad of subtle and not so subtle ways. . . . Consequently, our role changes from one "who knows everything" to one who may not know all the answers.

—RUTH DAVIDSON BELL

To realize the sacred power in

our relationships with one

another and to contend against

the forces that threaten to

damage and destroy us is to

bear luminous witness to the

goodness and power of God.

—CARTER HEYWARD

29

■

We pray for children who have no one to pray for them or protect and guide them.

—MARIAN WRIGHT EDELMAN

And then there is *intentional celebration.* I have known for a long time now that life is sustained when life is sacrament.

—CHRIS SMITH

29

monday
lunes
montag
lundi

Janine Bentivegna, *Expecting,*

© 1997, photograph

■

Women are the gateway to the world, a child can't even enter the world except by a woman. A woman is a powerful creature.

—LURLINE J. BAKER-KENT

30

God rejoices in that he is
our Mother.

—JULIAN OF NORWICH

■

When I look at some of the men I meet, it seems that

what they needed to learn when they were boys isn't to

be found at the office. It's an interior world, of intimacy,

of connection. It's a world in which being a father is as

important—and as time-consuming—as being a mother, and

the most pressing business of our lives is our relationships.

—ANNA QUINDLEN

I want to have children, I believe in that whole generativity and needing to leave something behind, I guess. Bringing a child into the world—I can't think of anything more wonderful or more beautiful than that.

—JANE GREATHOUSE

30

saturday

sábado

samstag

samedi

■

The truest direction comes from inside. I give the most strength to my children by being willing to look within myself, and by being honest with them about what I find there. . . . In this way they begin to learn to look beyond their own fears.

—AUDRE LORDE

238

The omnipresent daily
details of those mother
years, which seemed so
pressing then . . . I only
wish now that I'd savored
them all more, at the time.

—BETTY FRIEDAN

30

Betsy Molnar, *Sunshine with Jonah,*

© 1995, photograph

■

There is a pregnant knowing that viscerally experiences
the incomprehensible actuality of new life. . . . All of us
know the origin of this pregnant truth somewhere deep
within, for we are all potentially vessels of life.

—WENDY M. WRIGHT

31

When we can participate

fully in the process of our

lives, we discover new

forms of our creative self.

—ANNE WILSON SCHAEF

■

Shared responsibility for child care can happen in small
community settings where people know and trust one
another. It cannot happen in those settings if parents
regard children as their "property," their "possession."

—BELL HOOKS

Sometimes our near-grown

children become our teachers

as they introduce us to new

approaches to old problems

and as they help us, or force us,

to explore our long-held values

and beliefs about such things

as politics, religion, life styles,

and sexuality.

—JEANNE JACOBS SPEIZER

31

■

Most important was the sense that we were all engaged

in a process of growth, teenager and adult, searching

for answers, uncovering even more questions.

—CAROLINA MANCUSO

In the incarnation, Jesus

comes among us to help us

learn how to live in this

wilderness, as the animals

do, and to make it all

sacred, holy.

—GENEVA M. BUTZ

31

monday
lunes
montag
lundi

Mona Gazala Solymos,

Painless, detail of installation,

© 1997, assemblage

tuesday
martes
dienstag
mardi

■

If we have a moral obligation in these times, it is to be joyful in the face of what we know. . . . But we are also called to be midwives for what is being born.

—ELIZABETH ROBERTS

250

32

The *choice* to have a child makes the whole experience of motherhood different, and the choice to be generative in other ways can at last be made, and is being made by many women now, without guilt.

—BETTY FRIEDAN

■

As a girl, I knew that someday I would have children. My
closest models, my mother and my grandmother, had
both had children and also had used their minds and had
careers in the public world. So I had no doubt that, whatever career I might choose, I would have children, too.

—MARGARET MEAD

I am the mother of both a son
and a daughter. While I love
them equally with a passion of
stunning intensity, I know the
love takes different shapes.

—CAROLE KLEIN

32

■

Perhaps one of the most excruciating struggles to us as
parents of grownups is that of figuring out how much we
can say, suggest, or do to influence children who we
feel are making hurtful decisions.

—ALICE JUDSON RYERSON AND
WENDY COPPEDGE SANFORD

Having been gathered by
love, we are sent back to
our everyday world to share
love, not as a sentimental
feeling but in caring actions.

—LAVON BAYLER

32

33

monday
lunes
montag
lundi

Janine Bentivegna, *Untitled,*

© 1996, Polaroid transfer

■

We pray for ourselves . . . that we will help solve rather than cause the problems our children face, by struggling to be worthy of emulation, since we teach each minute by example.

—MARIAN WRIGHT EDELMAN

33

Mothers are the lives

which move education.

    —Frances E. Harper

■

Focusing on ourselves as parents has helped us shrug
that superparent off our shoulders, to accept our
imperfections.

—WENDY COPPEDGE SANFORD

Surely part of our personhood
is defined by that powerful
experience as mother, which is
far more than mystique. It is a
sort of heavy joyous-painful
shadow, under and over everything else we do during those
mother years.

—BETTY FRIEDAN

33

How do we then make friends with our stretch marks, our varicose veins, our stomach in pregnancy or the pendulous breasts we're going to have when we nurse our babies?

—JOAN SHEINGOLD DITZION AND

DENNIE PALMER WOLF

The women's movement has changed how women see themselves, their relationships with men, and what they want for their children.

—BONNIE WATKINS AND

NINA ROTHCHILD

33

monday
lunes
montag
lundi

Deborah Pinter, Sorrow, © 1996,

photograph

■

Whether or not we ever experience physical pregnancy,

God calls us to give birth to the holy in our lives.

—Jan L. Richardson

34

For adults who don't already have children of their own, the decision to live with another person's children has special complexities.

—RUTH DAVIDSON BELL

So often, we are stuck in the amazing belief that it is our responsibility to *teach* our children. We forget that it is equally important to *learn* from them.

—ANNE WILSON SCHAEF

Like children pressed to the
breast or cradled in arms,
we come to know the tender
presence of our God.

—WENDY M. WRIGHT

34

■

Wisdom is a kind of knowledge based on intuition,

but the intuition, in turn, comes from living and being in

touch with the range of experience long life offers.

—MARIA HARRIS

The kind, loving mother
who knows and sees the
need of her child guards it
very tenderly.

—Julian of Norwich

34

Marilyn C. Szalay, Games, © 1982,

photograph

■

Women have been trying to balance multiple claims and

demands from before the beginning of history, for

women's work has always embraced the array of tasks

that can be done simultaneously with caring for a child.

—MARY CATHERINE BATESON

35

As our children explore

further from us, we see

them completing a major

phase in their lifelong

process of becoming

themselves.

—JEANNE JACOBS SPEIZER

thursday

jueves

donnerstag

jeudi

■

For you formed my inward parts,

you knit me together in my mother's womb.

—Psalm 139:13

You can plant the seeds, but you really can't predict the outcome. You can do only what you think best and you have to keep on believing in the process.

—CAROLINA MANCUSO

35

■

Our children must never lose their zeal for building a better world.

—MARY MCLEOD BETHUNE

Children are not born with a
defined set of moral values.
They need clearly explained
rules to enable them to
adjust and contribute to the
society into which they have
been catapulted.

—JANE GOODALL

35

week **36**

monday
lunes
montag
lundi

Nanette Yannuzzi Maciás,

Umbilicus: Remnants and

Huaraches, detail from installation,

© 1996, sumi ink on piano rolls

■

Letting our children go is something that has to happen
inside us.

—ALICE JUDSON RYERSON AND

WENDY COPPEDGE SANFORD

36

Jesus Christ, who does

good as opposed to evil,

is our true Mother.

—JULIAN OF NORWICH

thursday
jueves
donnerstag
jeudi

∎

A parent often wonders what lessons her child will remember. Other teachers must wonder too. As with parenting, it probably is not what one would expect.

—JUDY SCOTT RICHARDSON

284

Without stories a woman is lost when she comes to make the important decisions of her life. She does not learn to value her struggles, to celebrate her strengths, to comprehend her pain. Without stories she cannot understand herself.

—CAROL P. CHRIST AND CHARLENE SPRETNAK

36

■

Ultimately, it all comes down to love. Not the sugary
kind; love fierce and creative enough to demand
change—for ourselves, our children, and the planet.
That's the "mother love" I aspire to.

—ROBIN MORGAN

I see the sun sinking toward

the horizon. The colors of

the sunset are gorgeous.

There's a road approaching

the sunset and I'm walking

along the road, stopping to

look at things beside the

path, and finding each more

beautiful than the one

before.

—MARIA HARRIS

36

■

JANINE BENTIVEGNA, a graduate of the Cooper School of Art, operates a successful commercial photography business in Cleveland Heights, Ohio. Recently, her work was included in *Pictures from the Edge,* a nationally touring show illuminating the issue of homelessness.

JANET CENTURY, an assignment photographer from Cleveland, Ohio, travels throughout the United States and Europe documenting diverse communities and the human condition. Her personal work focuses on figurative subjects.

ANNE HERSCH, a senior at Cleveland Heights High School, is a local and national award-winner at both student and professional shows. She studies photography with Betsy Molnar and has experience in studio shooting with Kalman and Pabst Photo Group. Anne lives with her family in Cleveland Heights, Ohio.

KRISSI KAHOUN, a freelance photographer from Cleveland, Ohio, recently graduated from the Colorado Institute of Art. One of Krissi's works, a Polaroid transfer, appears on the cover of this journal. Her inclusion in this collection has inspired her thanks to her mother for giving her birth.

NANETTE YANNUZZI MACÍAS teaches sculpture and installation at Oberlin College in Oberlin, Ohio. Nanette uses a variety of materials, from found objects to photography, video, and sound to investigate the female body as the site for identity, reproduction, poetry, memory, and loss. Her work has appeared in New York, Mexico, California, and Venezuela.

BETSY MOLNAR, a Cleveland fine artist, is owner of Big Stills, a custom
black-and-white photo lab specializing in large-format work that
serves the commercial and fine art market. Betsy is recognized for
her technical skills and creative abstracts and figurative works.

DEBORAH PINTER is an art therapist in Cleveland, Ohio. Over the last year
she created dramatic black-and-white photographs of women posed
in a classical style imitating a nineteenth-century funeral statue of a
woman. Deborah sought to convey a variety of emotions in the
poses, such as grief, peace, and longing.

SARAH C. SCHUSTER is an associate professor of art at Oberlin College,
Oberlin, Ohio. Over the last decade her work has focused on issues
of fertility and infertility, reflecting the complicated relationship
between biological creation and artistic creation. In January 1995
her show entitled *ms. conceptions* opened at the Ceres Gallery in
New York City.

MARILYN C. SZALAY, a Cleveland-based artist, photographer, and art edu-
cator, describes her life and vision as a single journey. She is grateful to the many women who have opened themselves to her camera,
allowing her to express her own experience through their eyes.

MONA GAZALA SOLYMOS, a lover of books and history, creates assem-
blages that incorporate the printed word with imagery from books,
photo albums, and ancient archetypes that highlight the cycles of
life: birth, death, and continuity through the generations.